'Shortt is one of the UK's most though
gious commentators.'

Professor Michael Barnes SJ,
formerly Reader in Interreligious Relations,
Heythrop College, University of London

'A triumph of ambition and concision.'

Lucy Beckett, author of In the Light of Christ:
Writings in the Western Tradition

'Argued with elegance and authority . . . refreshing and highly enjoyable.'

Melvyn Bragg, writer and broadcaster

'Are the world's major religions forces for good or harm? Rupert Shortt provides a fascinating and enlightening discussion, summarizing key arguments on both sides, with a much-needed appeal for a deeper conversation about religion and secularism.'

Imam Dr Usama Hasan,
Head of Islamic Studies, Quilliam International

'To deliver a confident and unassailable answer to the question, "Does religion do more harm than good?" would require a complete record of every act motivated by religion in human history and a corresponding record of their consequences, which is about as impossible an undertaking as the mind could imagine. Which is why this debate will continue unabated and unresolved till the end of time. That said, this book is a welcome addition to the irresolvable conflict. Coming from within the religious tradition, its generous and self-critical tone makes as strong a case as possible for the good religion does, in however long the run. But no matter where you are coming from on the issue, it will certainly make you think.'

'An admirably concise, thoughtful and fair discussion of the virtues and vices of a religious society.'

'An original and challenging reply to the assumption that religion will or should wither away in the face of secular fundamentalism.'

'I love this book. It demolishes fashionable atheists who claim religion only does harm. It criticizes extremists of all faiths who promote hatred and violence in the name of religion, and it praises, with caveats, those who seek meaning in their lives within a community, find something in the transcendent, and want to make the world a better place. Strong arguments, tersely put, lead to a conclusion that gives those seeking and respecting human dignity the benefit of the doubt – for they are on a journey where religion can do more good than harm.'

Rupert Shortt is religion editor of *The Times Literary Supplement* and a former Visiting Fellow at the University of Oxford. His books include *Benedict XVI* (2005), *Christianophobia: A Faith under Attack* (2012), *Rowan's Rule: The Biography of the Archbishop* (2014) and *God Is No Thing: Coherent Christianity* (2016).

DOES RELIGION DO MORE HARM THAN GOOD?

RUPERT SHORTT

First published in Great Britain in 2019

Society for Promoting Christian Knowledge
36 Causton Street
London SW1P 4ST
www.spck.org.uk

British Library Cataloguing-in-Publication Data
A catalogue record for this book is available from the British Library

ISBN 978–0–281–07871–4
eBook ISBN 978–0–281–07872–1

1 3 5 7 9 10 8 6 4 2

Typeset by Manila Typesetting Company
Printed in Great Britain by Jellyfish Print Solutions

eBook by Manila Typesetting Company

Produced on paper from sustainable forests

For Bernice and David Martin

Contents

Preface

Any claim that faith differences – and the badges of identity they reflect – might prove as divisive in the twenty-first century as political creeds were throughout the twentieth would have prompted derision in many quarters as recently as the 1990s. Then, of course, a paradox suddenly turned into a platitude. The awareness forms one of the more sobering rationales for this book. Mercifully, others proved far more constructive. Few distinctions matter more than that between good and bad religion.

I am very grateful to Philip Law for entrusting me with the project. His constant support has meant a lot – as has the kindness and professionalism of his colleagues at SPCK, especially Amy Carothers, Rima Devereaux and Rhoda Hardie. Grants were generously awarded by the Porticus Trust and the John Booth Charitable Foundation.

For advice, feedback and other forms of sustenance, I am indebted to Stig Abell, Mary Beard, Jonathan Benthall, Clare Carlisle, Felipe Fernández-Armesto,

Arnold Hunt, Robert Irwin, Maren Meinhardt, James Orr, Thomas Small, Alvin Uzcanga and Oscar Yuill.

Rupert Shortt
London

1

Grasping the question

The world swarms with self-appointed experts on religion. A leading sociologist such as David Martin has noted that few matters are as heatedly debated – and pronounced on at a moment's notice – as the relationship between faith and culture. When I was invited to answer the question posed in the title of this book, responses from a gallery of figures in journalism, academia and on the street proved tellingly confident. Consider the following, which represents my own summaries of two widely held views.

Religion does more harm than good because it is based on dubious speculation, often imposed in authoritarian ways, about what cannot be known in principle. Since there are no earthly scales capable of weighing questions relating to our final source and destiny (if any), it is better to abandon a flawed project and get on with living a decent life in the here and now.

Religion does more good than harm because the major faiths set the experience of human beings – who are often selfish or destructive but also potentially noble – against a transcendent horizon. In this broader perspective believers can face the future with courage and hope, learning among much else that life is worth living responsibly, because it has ultimate meaning.

That religion does more harm than good is especially clear in our age of growing 'endarkenment'. Blasphemy has re-emerged as a hot-button issue in the West, as well as less tolerant societies. It is not only enforced by Muslims who kill cartoonists and denounce Ayaan Hirsi Ali, a victim of female genital mutilation, as a rabble-rouser. Toxic Islamists resemble the toxic Christians who were once as intolerant as any al-Qaeda or Daesh terrorist today. The sword has been the shadow of the cross for much of Christian history. Islam has its own variants of the Emperor Constantine's notorious slogan *in hoc signo vinces*. And although they are the worst offenders by dint of their size and missionary thrust, the world's two largest faiths are not a special case. The trouble really centres on religion as such – or the lion's share of it. Right now, Hindu mobs are oppressing non-Hindus in South Asia for not sharing their outlook and thus not being 'authentically' Indian; Buddhists are displaying allied forms of chauvinism in Burma and Sri Lanka. Any reasonably open-minded person will grant that the great spiritual traditions preach worthy ideals for the most part. But they also create in-groups and out-groups by definition. So when faith isn't directly responsible for poisoning the wells of discourse and public life, it can itself be poisoned by them. Land grabs, shrill nationalism and other mainly political evils become more pernicious still when sanctified by angry little gods. What's more, false claims to infallibility come in many forms. In North America and Europe, the antics of no-platforming, trigger-warning thought police on social media represent religion transposed into a secular key. Trial by Twitter recalls the Salem witch hunts. Lastly, there is an unbridgeable chasm between religion and science.

That religion does more good than harm is especially clear in its status as our best hope in neo-pagan times. Almost all past societies have acknowledged and cultivated the spiritual dimension; for well over a century, scepticism about faith has fed a wider spurning of goodness, beauty and truth. Godless modern mores were not only seen in the horrors of Auschwitz, the gulag or Mao's China. They are also reflected in moral relativism, crass consumerism, large-scale family breakdown, drug abuse and the sexualization of children. Opponents of faith should be careful what they wish for. The secular liberal state now claims more than its due, including the right to govern a citizen's conscience and set norms as though the government were the only force in society that mattered. Authentic religion offers richer visions of a just humanity. The coarsening of what passes for debate both on and off the internet marks a further rejection of such visions. Much journalism misrepresents faith because it alights on today's news at the expense of deeper currents. Reporters tell us about sudden volcanic eruptions, but not the steady, barely noticed irrigation supplied by underground streams. Humanity is not the measure of all things. The two pearls of greatest price in most people's lives are love and happiness. Neither can be commodified; neither is to be attained directly. The best mapping of this mysterious terrain comes in the major religions. Of course they can be put to corrupt use. Faith is like fire: it warms, but it can also burn. And just like heat, spiritual allegiance contributes greatly to our flourishing under the right conditions. The benefits have been intellectual as well as social. Whatever hotheads on either side of the debate may think, claims of a genuine clash between religion and science are illusory.

These two sets of replies are of course sharply opposed. Other responses I heard are harder to categorize. A historian pointed out that religion is an aspect of culture, 'so asking whether religion does more harm than good is as futile as asking the same question about culture'. John Lennon's invitation to 'imagine no religion' thus betrays a basic misunderstanding of what religion is. You can guess at what the world might look like if Al Gore had become President of the United States, or Germany had won the First World War. But asking how things might be if religion (or culture) had never existed is a counterfactual speculation too far. This insight strikes me as crucial. Although I hope that what follows will shed light on the merits and drawbacks associated with spiritual belief, the elusiveness of my theme should be underlined at the start.

A Buddhist thought the answer simple: 'It all depends on the practitioner. Faith can make good people better and bad people worse.' A philosopher questioned whether there is any such thing as 'religion' outside the minds of opportunistic or maybe soft-headed public servants:

> Religion in the abstract does not exist. No one apart from politicians voices allegiance to it. It's just a catch-all term devised by eighteenth-century rationalists to label the superstitions of the vulgar masses who weren't like them. The creeds of the major faiths are in any case mutually contradictory. So if any religion is true, then most religions are false.

A squadron of atheists told me in terms leaving no room for doubt that faith is profoundly harmful through fomenting violence as well as being a social and mental straitjacket. More than one quoted Pascal's dictum that men never do evil so completely and cheerfully as when they act from religious conviction. Evidence for the prosecution in the continuing suit of secularism vs God is familiar: Galileo; the Inquisition; witch-burning; young-earth creationism; Christian anti-Judaism causing or feeding evils including the blood libel, *The Protocols of the Elders of Zion*, pogroms and the Holocaust; religiously based gender discrimination and homophobia; the melancholy statistic that Islamist fanatics are responsible for most global terrorism today; the arrogance and cruelty of so many missionaries (see the testimony of witnesses from Rousseau to Kipling to Lévi-Strauss), especially those convinced that unconverted 'heathens' would burn in hell for all eternity.

Lastly, a Christian theologian with an open-handed attitude to faith in general praised what she sees as the richest articulation of the human spirit:

Interest in the flourishing of all beings has been placed on the moral agenda of most religious traditions. It is religion which can promote the honing of virtue and offer the securest embedding of moral community. Alongside the humanist dimension, faith adds a rationale for commitment to freedom and dignity. Believers have come to see life as a freely bestowed gift, and so to open up to a calling from outside themselves to accept divine mercy and make it real for others.

Later in my exchange with the historian he added an important caveat, pointing out that religion is not an abstract noun. It involves sets of relationships between people who are typically agreed about basic beliefs, or at least some core set of commitments about ritual practice. Being a human practice, it can be used for good or ill. So can medicine, for that matter. There are doctors who have used their skill to help torturers do a better job.

These comments strike me as the shrewdest to have emerged from my straw poll. My agreement with the philosopher was more qualified. In one sense his insight was wholly valid. Viewed from a wide angle as it has unfolded over millennia, religion is certainly very hard to define. It would include rites in the ancient world, such as animal and human sacrifice, employed as forms of scapegoating. But to dwell at any length in such territory during a brief overview would be eccentric. We are here concerned with global faiths that have produced major bodies of critical thought, and with markers given by the sociology of religion, which sees its subject as involving an apprehension and symbolic representation of sacred or non-ordinary reality. Scholars in this field remind us that human beings do not merely investigate the natural world at a scientific level. We also seek to make sense of our lives via all sorts of evolutionary adaptations – agriculture, dance, literature – that have emerged from animal play, animal empathy, ritual and myth, during a long history of tribal societies without much sense of the beyond, through supernatural king-god monarchies, to more recent societies with their religions of value transcending the brute givens of existence.

With this arc in mind, we might point up developments during the first millennium BCE. Whether or not one accepts the term 'Axial Age' to encompass this period, it can nevertheless be described as transformational. The ideal was contrasted with the real; visionary horizons of hope were set against the frustrations of the everyday world. Though expressed in different idioms across the world, the quest for transcendence – a higher dimension of reality embodying more exalted values – arose in China, through reflection on the way of nature; in India, through worldly renunciation; in Israel, through prophetic denunciation; and in Greece, through theoretical reflection and the quest for wisdom.

Critics (including those who would kick away the apparently superfluous spiritual ladders that have raised us to the branches we now perch on) may nevertheless remain unmoved by these points, for at least two sorts of reason. The first is practical. Context matters, they may say, but so does the big picture. To wit: harmony between the major religions remains a remote goal; the destabilizing effects of Islamist extremism especially can be seen far from the Middle East or Ground Zero in New York. The recent, much-noted 'return of religion' across societies including Egypt, Turkey and India (a sharp reaction against secularizing drives in these countries several generations ago) supplies fresh grounds for disquiet. Formerly secular challenges such as the confrontation between Israel and the Palestinians have taken on an overtly religious cast; religion has played a role in recent and continuing civil wars from Sri Lanka to Chechnya to Sudan. Along or near the tenth parallel of latitude north of the equator, between Nigeria and Indonesia and the Philippines, religious fervour and political unrest are reinforcing each other. Other faith-based political groups, whether violent or not, are justly seen as highly divisive by their critics. They include Vishwa Hindu Parishad in India (which sowed the seeds of Hindu nationalism reaped by the BJP during the 1990s), the Muslim Brotherhood in Egypt and Jordan, Hamas in the Palestinian territories, Hezbollah in Lebanon, the Nahdlatul Ulama in Indonesia, and the Zionist Christian movement in the United States, which supports illegal Israeli settlements in the West Bank.

But are these prosecution arguments so much stronger than those voiced by the defence? I am not just referring to the obvious point that religion is (whatever else) the world's greatest source of social capital, or that faith-based conviction has mobilized millions of people to oppose authoritarian regimes, inaugurate democratic transitions, support human rights and relieve human suffering. I am also talking about the painstaking sociological analysis that disentangles the causes of a given conflict – demonstrating, for example, how often faith is politicized, and thus how the notionally 'religious' roots of a given conflict are really social problems in disguise. The Troubles

in Ireland bear this out. A well-known gag tells of
a man being stopped at a roadblock and asked by the
guard about his religion. He answers that he is an
atheist. 'Protestant or Catholic atheist?' comes the
reply. In his influential polemic *God Is Not Great*,[1]
Christopher Hitchens sees deep significance in the
guard's quip. It apparently shows that an 'obsession'
with religion 'rotted even the legendary local sense of
humour'. More careful observers see that it is Hitchens
who misses the force of the joke, which is really about
identity. As the atheist philosopher Tim Crane has
argued, the guard's question suggests 'not that religion
is the immovable force in the conflict but that actual
belief in God is irrelevant. What matters is what group
you belong to.'[2]

This insight applies much more widely. The roman-
tic nationalism underlying so much conflict over the
past 200 years derives from history, ethnicity and lin-
guistic diversity, as well as from religion. Singling out
faith-based motivation for acts of violence is irrational, because weapons are used in the name of an
alleged greater good all the time. Islamist suicide
bombers have learnt their deadly craft from secular
exemplars. The roots of contemporary terrorism lie

more in radical ideologies like Leninism, incubated in the West, than in religion. Across other parts of the world, faith allegiances often shade into ethnic divides, which in turn merge with claims to land, water and oil.

Or consider the examples of the Balkans and the Caucasus, where religion can exacerbate differences that are fundamentally political. As I have noted elsewhere,[3] this theme cries out to be placed in the broader context of nineteenth-century and postcolonial nationalism. For example, numerous Christian subjects of the Ottoman sultan thirsted for independence and a freer expression of their culture. But their chief inspirations included Napoleon and the nationalist movements he spearheaded. We can thus find many examples of conflicts in which adherents of the same faith are enemies, just as other cases where two religions can be aligned together. It is telling that Raymond Aron's classic study *Peace and War*[4] scarcely mentions religion at all.

The Crusades and the Thirty Years War (1618–48) are naturally central exhibits in debate about religion and violence. But far more attention should be paid to the rise of the nation state and the homogenizing force exerted on often unwilling populations by politically driven nationalist rulers. In his book *The Myth of Religious Violence*,[5] William T. Cavanaugh cites Charles Tilly's remark that 'war made the state and the state made war'. He also quotes Gabriel Ardant to the effect that in the process of state-building, the most serious source of violence – and the greatest spur to the growth of the state – was the attempt to collect taxes from an unwilling populace. Violence also sprang from opposition among local elites to the centralizing efforts of monarchs. No wonder co-religionists might find themselves on opposite sides of political divides.

A contemporary example in a related field is instructive. Sarah Eltantawi's book *Shar'iah on Trial*[6] centres on the case of Amina Lawal, the Nigerian woman sentenced to death by stoning in 2001 for conceiving a child out of wedlock. Her case drew international attention. Initially convinced that Lawal's vile treatment could only be ascribed to a barbarous theology, Eltantawi came by degrees to see the story more in terms of Nigeria's politics than of Islam as such. The lesson she learnt was encapsulated almost a millennium ago by a thinker such as Al-Ghazali, who observed that

Islamic jurisprudence is one-tenth text and nine-tenths context.

The factors rehearsed in the past few paragraphs ought to unsettle at least part of the story told by hardline secularists. Karen Armstrong rightly protests against a certain cast of mind when she notes that all sorts and conditions of people ('American commentators and psychiatrists, London taxi drivers and Oxford academics') blame undifferentiated 'religion' for all the major wars in history. While important, however, the counter-arguments do not necessarily defeat the secularists, because of a second, theoretical, rejection of religion underlying their empirical one. Many cannot accept an analogy between religion and other forms of kinship bond. In their eyes, tribe, ethnicity, language and so on all at least boil down to something real – unlike religion, which only trades in dangerous falsehoods. That is why we have an issue in the first place. Take a more tangible comparison. There is plenty of scope for grown-up disagreement over the pros and cons of veganism. But there is no serious discussion to be had about the alleged benefits of crack cocaine. Readers of Gibbon will recall his remark about how sacred rituals were viewed in the

Roman Empire: as true by the ignorant masses, as false by the philosophers and, by the magistrates, as a convenient means of social control. Gibbon's successors can thus be forgiven for thinking that men and women come of age have outgrown the fantasies of yesteryear, whether or not religion's role in fomenting conflict is exaggerated.

These thoughts propel us on to philosophical terrain. If you believe atheism to be true, then you are of course likely to conclude that religion is inherently bogus (no matter how much good done in its name by default), for the simple reason that it rests on false beliefs. There are historical questions relevant to our theme that need airing, including how much this or that faith has encouraged widely recognized goods such as scientific enquiry or freedom of conscience or democracy and the rule of law. Are religious believers – Christians especially – disingenuous to claim credit for providing the theoretical ecosystems apparently needed for advances that would have occurred anyway? Conversely, are opponents of religion wrong-headed in failing to see that so much of what they think of as common sense available to 'neutral' reason actually rests on unacknowledged theological foundations? This factor applies to many scientific developments as much as to landmark documents from Magna Carta (anchored in biblical norms) to Milton's *Areopagitica* to the UN Declaration of Human Rights, which was largely crafted by Protestants. Copernicus, Descartes, Leibniz, Newton and other authors of the scientific revolution were not just passive products of a Christian culture, but serious believers with theological expertise to match their commitments to mathematics and physics.

As indicated, though, such issues are logically preceded by a deeper question, namely whether religious belief has a rational basis in the first place. Hard-headed thinking is certainly called for. But our enquiry should note the limits of wholly disengaged analysis. In other words, we must also attend to how faith is mapped from within. Having conceded an important point to the anti-religion camp, we should in fairness make an equally important concession to the other side. The nutritional analogy remains useful up to a point. While vegans are not the only people entitled to voice opinions about the merits of their diet, they do possess a special warrant for commenting on what it *feels* like to avoid all animal products – especially if they speak with the benefit of some scientific knowledge.

Note, too, where this comparison breaks down. In a debate for and against veganism, all informed participants will at least agree over what it is they disagree about. Yet it is because thoughtful believers often do *not* recognize the models of religion regularly peddled by secularists that we cannot even begin our main discussion without substantial ground-clearing. For example, people of faith regularly insist that the deity rejected by Richard Dawkins is more an inflated creature than the God of classical theism. (Dawkins even makes the surreal claim that our putative creator would need to have evolved by natural selection.[7]) The psychologist Oliver Sacks, raised in an Orthodox Jewish household, lost his faith as a schoolboy after a prayer experiment.[8] He planted two rows of radishes, cursing one and blessing the other, before concluding that religion was a sham when both grew equally well. Did this disprove the existence of God, or merely discredit the simplistic claims Sacks had been taught? Atheists can plainly score cheap rhetorical victories by lampooning the ignorance or charlatanism of certain believers, just as some people might dismiss veganism out of hand because certain vegans are malnourished, or others might avoid swimming entirely on the basis that it carries a risk of drowning. But to win an argument convincingly, you need the backbone to confront a robust version of the contrary position. In our case, this means that it is essential to probe stronger arguments for faith, and the patterns of life to which thoughtful as well as hot-headed believers are rightly or wrongly committing themselves. This is hardly to draw premature conclusions. It is simply a bid to match our tools to the task in hand. After all, would anyone take seriously a discussion of whether socialism does more harm than good by ignoring Western Europe and instead focusing only on Cuba and the Khmer Rouge?

2

Spiritual paths in theory and practice

W e have already noted rising levels of religious belief worldwide. Three-quarters of humanity profess a faith; the figure is projected to reach the 80 per cent mark by 2050 – not just because believers tend to have more children, but also through the spread of democracy.[1] Significant, too, is the growing prominence of post-secular thinking in several disciplines. The landscape looked very different as recently as the 1980s. Influential commentators assumed that mainstream religion would fade away within a few generations; anglophone theologians, to name only one group, were often intellectually insecure. In a different setting such as Latin America, Marxism furnished the conceptual tools used by a posse of distinguished Catholics crafting a 'theology of liberation'. This movement faced shal-

low criticism from some conservatives. Its more searching critics did not doubt that questionable power
structures merited serious critique drawing on eco-
nomics or the social sciences. But they also saw that
a vital issue centred on whether theology itself could
be a conversation partner with something original to
say independently of other world views.

The turning of the tide is a significant chapter in
the history of ideas meriting a full-length study of its
own.[2] Though the trend cannot be discussed at length
here, its main conclusions are worth outlining.
The scales of debate on whether religion does more
harm than good will tilt a bit if the theistic picture
looks more coherent on closer inspection than
many had previously thought, and naturalism – the
belief that everything is ultimately explicable in the
language of natural science – less plausible as a con-
sequence.

For example, a student embarking on a philosophy
of religion course today might typically be told that
there are six strong arguments for the existence of God:

- the modal ontological argument[3]
- the kalām cosmological argument[4]

- the argument from moral truths[5]
- the argument from mathematical truths[6]
- the argument from fine-tuning[7]
- the argument from consciousness.[8]

None of these should be seen as logically coercive, but that does not render them redundant. If such forms of reasoning can draw one towards the threshold of belief – to the point where one makes a life-changing commitment, moving beyond intellectual assent alone – or if they can build bridges with atheism, demonstrating that religion is not irrational, then they will have served a valid purpose. Believers seeking a more straightforward rationale for their convictions interlacing reason and faith could cite three forms of awareness: first, that we are embodied beings with the capacity to grasp meaning and truth; second, that our status is to be viewed as a gift prompting awe, gratitude and a heightened sense of ethical responsibility; third, an acknowledgement of this gift as grounded in a reality that freely bestows itself on us.

We can also note that divine transcendence is pictured in broadly complementary ways across the major faiths. The conception I have in mind can be found in various forms of pagan belief deriving from late antiquity, such as Neoplatonism; in the three Abrahamic religions; in Vedantic and Bhaktic Hinduism; in Sikhism; in some aspects of both Taoism and Mahayana Buddhist visions of Buddha Nature. They all tend to see God as the one infinite source of all reality: uncreated, eternal, omnipotent, omnipresent, transcending all things and, precisely by dint of not competing for space with creation, immanent to all things as well. From this standpoint, it is not even appropriate to say that God exists if by 'existence' we mean that God shares a property with created being. Better, rather, to say that God has uncreated being, or is being itself: the absolute on which the contingent relies at every moment.

In at least some major strands of Indian religious thought, God is described as infinite being, infinite consciousness and infinite bliss – *sat, chit* and *ananda* in Sanskrit – from whom we derive our existence and in whom we are to achieve ultimate fulfilment. St Gregory of Nyssa, the fourth-century Christian theologian, describes the divine life as an eternal act of knowledge and love, in which the God who is infinite being is also a boundless expression of consciousness, knowing himself as infinitely good and so also as an infinite outpouring of love. David Bentley Hart notes that a medieval Sufi thinker such as Ibn Arabi draws attention to the shared root of the terms *wujud* (being), *wijdan* (consciousness) and *wajd* (bliss) to designate God's mystical knowledge. Hart sees that these terms also encapsulate the ways in which several faiths picture the believer's own appropriation of the reality of God:

> For to say that God is being, consciousness, and bliss is also to say that he is the one reality in which all our existence, knowledge and love subsist, from which they come and to which they go, and that therefore he is somehow present in even our simplest experience of the world, and is approachable by way of contemplative and moral refinement of that experience. That is to say, these three words are not only a metaphysical explanation of God, but also a phenomenological explanation of the human encounter with God.[9]

This model need form no challenge at all to the integrity of science, notwithstanding ignorant, authoritarian voices in parts of the Muslim and Christian worlds who oppose the teaching of evolution in schools among other subjects. To show why, some commentators have given the example of a basic act such as heating water on a stove to illustrate the difference between what is technically known as primary and secondary causation. According to classical monotheistic teaching, the process has been misconceived by believers and non-believers alike in three ways. The first mistake is to suppose that the gas heats the water and God is not involved at all; the second, that God heats the water and the gas plays no part; the third, that God makes the gas act on the water as a puppeteer moves a puppet, meaning that the gas does not exercise a power of its own. The Abrahamic faiths take a more nuanced view. As a canvas supports a painting, so God makes the whole situation to exist: the gas, its power and its action on the water. God and the gas work at different levels, not in competition. Creation is thus seen as a relationship of radical dependence. To cite an insight deriving from St Thomas Aquinas, God's creation of the world should not be likened to a carpenter making a chest. A better analogy would be more intimate – a singer performing a song, for instance. The difference is profound. Carpenter and chest are discrete entities. Carpenters can pass on the articles they make, never seeing them again. But a song is by definition an emanation of a singer.

If we absorb these points, it becomes clearer why the doctrine of creation as classically framed cannot be undermined by Darwin's theories. Aubrey Moore was right to say that 'Darwin appeared, and, under the guise of a foe, did the work of a friend', because he held that God had made a world that makes itself. Another pious misconception, especially common in the Islamic world, leads people to forswear insurance – and even preventive measures such as equipping ships with lifeboats – on the basis that any disastrous event would be the will of God. That such attitudes are highly damaging ought to be self-evident. But for those who don't see them as forming grounds to throw out the baby of faith with the bathwater of misinterpretation, the answer to bad theology is the good sort, not no theology at all.

Other aspects of a more rigorous theological framework deserve a mention. Some conservative believers have taken a dim view of all human activity that does not have a specific religious shape. But a major strand of Christianity, Thomism (itself an edifice resting on the foundation of fruitful exchanges between Jews, Muslims and Christians), maintains that nature has its own integrity because it reflects the rationality of the Creator. In the fullness of time creatures have evolved with the capacity to think, receive and process information, and to reason about their place in the world as a whole.

From this we may infer that an open-handed believer in one tradition has solid grounds for supposing that other spiritual paths may be approximating to this or that aspect of truth. The global faiths are usually speci-fied as Judaism, Christianity, Islam, Hinduism, Buddhism and Sikhism. Even if we granted that one of these six (or another) embodies a definitive disclosure of the truth of our being, that should not imply that all other religions are meaningless. Islam, for example, though considering itself the vessel of God's final reve-lation in the Qur'an, nevertheless explicitly teaches that Judaism and Christianity in particular contain sig-nificant elements of the truth. Several Mughal rulers of India extended this concentric model to include Hindus, who were also classed as 'People of the Book' alongside Christians and Jews, because of their Scriptures. Christianity's presentation of the workings of grace beyond the visible Church may be deduced from John 14.6 ('I am the way, and the truth, and the life. No one comes to the Father except through me'). Though this is seen both by certain believers and their critics as an exclusivist proof text – you cannot be saved unless you're a Christian – the opposite interpretation is valid. 'Me' refers to the Word of God, God's reason and wisdom, which, as the Prologue of John's Gospel makes clear, enlightens all people. The insight itself echoes earlier biblical teaching that humanity is made in the divine image.

Several more inferences implied by these points should be outlined. Given that we are truth-seeking – and truth-*discovering* – beings, advances in empirical knowledge were bound to arise in the fullness of time. Religion can be more or less conducive to this process. Science prospered in Muslim and Christian societies (especially the latter) because of their faith in a Creator whose grounding of the intelligible world formed a focus for confidence in rational enquiry as such. This was no accident. That science developed at a slower rate in civilizations such as India is partly connected with the otherworldliness of Hinduism and Buddhism; that it has withered as well as thrived in the Islamic and Christian worlds at different times is certainly connected with the ebb and flow of contrasting theological tides.[10]

* * *

What of discipleship in practice? Many, of course, are uninterested in technical arguments about the existence of God or the theory of knowledge, focusing instead on how to live their lives. The patterns of altruistic giving associated with religion could all be grouped together as cultural instances of 'good works' (*kala erga*, in the New Testament's phrase). In Hindi, the notion of *dān* (giving) has resonances with the Bhagavad Gita and the principle of *dharma* (duty), while *seva* (selfless service) is similar to the Christian *diakonīa*. The anthropologist Jonathan Benthall notes that Islam 'has stimulated the process of deprovincialising the common assumption that charity is a monopoly of the Euro-American West'.[11] Resembling the Hebraic tithe, *Zakat* is a basic injunction in the Qur'an and one of the five pillars of Islam. On a wider scale, all the major faiths preach salutary messages to a world facing dire environmental problems, abiding (though rapidly falling) poverty, and the mixed consequences of globalization.

In acting as they do, believers are consciously or unconsciously echoing a concern seen in much ancient philosophy. Just as there are objective grounds for establishing whether a lion or a lamb is flourishing – if it is well fed, well integrated in its environment, and free of disease, for example – humans can be appraised in allied ways. Aristotle taught that we have natural needs and capacities, the fulfilment of which amounts to happiness.

A crucial difference between humans and other animals is equally plain. Genuinely fulfilled human lives involve further dimensions, including *dignity*, which is connected with the exercise of choice, and *virtue*, implying the need to stretch or transcend ourselves. G. K. Chesterton wrote that it makes little sense to upbraid a lion for not being properly lion-like: lions are lions. The same is not true of human beings. People everywhere have a striking idea that they ought to behave in certain 'humane' ways, but also an awareness that they do not in fact behave as they should. It is often noted that these two facts are the root of all clear thinking about ourselves and our world.

Against this background we can perhaps see the justice of claims made by preachers down the ages: that our challenge is to align ourselves to the good and grow in knowledge of it. I would not dream of suggesting that the process cannot go wrong, or that groups and institutions cannot become corrupt or moribund. Still less am I implying that they should escape scrutiny and just criticism. My suggestion is that, at their best, the spiritual paths concerned offer an overarching vision of wholeness encompassing the ethical and emotional spheres, as well as the rational. The insight is well encapsulated by the philosopher Clare Carlisle:

> For many religious practitioners . . . devotional and contemplative practices are ways to reach towards the transcendent, and possibly even touch it. Over time, these practices open up their minds and bodies, expand their receptivity, shift the horizon of what they can feel and understand. And after years of practice it may no longer seem strange or unnatural to perceive moments of grace, when the transcendent flows right through the middle of life.[12]

This comment partially answers a related question: why join a community of belief in the first place? Why can't you be 'spiritual' in isolation, with or without an overarching context of meaning? You can, of course.

You can also do much good. The Church, for example, has consistently taught that conscience is the exercise of reasoned judgement. But it is communities of conviction that hone the vision, provide due means of discernment, and get things done. So the Jewish thinker Jonathan Sacks describes religion as

> part of the ecology of freedom because it supports families, communities, charities, voluntary associations, active citizenship and concern for the common good. It is a key contributor to civil society, which is what holds us together without the coercive power of law. Without it we will depend entirely on the State, and when that happens we risk what J. L. Talmon called 'totalitarian democracy', which is what revolutionary France eventually became.[13]

Here we have a cogent argument against consigning faith to the purely private domain. In order to forestall resentment in what can become religious ghettos, a better way is available in the form of 'interactive pluralism', which encourages robust dialogue among faith communities and between them and the State. No one has received the whole truth 'as God sees it', so all have something to learn, and all are accountable.

Sacks makes clear that many (believers and their critics alike) err in applying secular assumptions about power in a religious context. The model of a deity with unconditional power can all too easily develop into a projection of a given set of human norms to be imposed willy-nilly on others. Much mainstream religion contains the antidote to its own poison, however, including through the belief that creation is itself a radical act of sharing. Divine power, which displays no anxiety or rivalry, is best conceived in terms of a liberty to let the other be. Critics have regularly complained that faith is associated with heteronomy (the brute imposition of law from the outside), and thus with intolerance. But if our spade-work in various parts of a large field has turned the soil effectively, then some large assumptions may need revisiting.

Rowan Williams, a Christian counterpart to Sacks, identifies four core constituents of religiously informed human maturity: the management of dependence and freedom, the educating of the passions, attitudes to time, and the acceptance of mortality.[14] The first of these connects with observations already made. The Enlightenment formed a protest against unaccountable authority, but at the price of enthroning the private autonomous individual as the final arbiter in questions of meaning and value. The result was yet another false binary. Religious believers can reply that while undue subservience is plainly bad, no one should be an island. We are not self-created; we have nothing we have not received; the very acquisition of language itself involves considerable acts of trust.

In reckoning with the divine, they might add, people of faith are acknowledging a world not made by us and an initiative that is not ours, to cite the French philosopher Paul Ricœur. This initiative can in turn be echoed or reflected by self-conscious creatures. Christians, Williams notes, are taught to think of themselves not just as growing into the divine life generally but as participating in the form of divine life represented by the divine Word or Son:

> Our human identity therefore becomes one in which we both acknowledge in prayer our dependence . . . and in acknowledging that dependence, we are empowered to do the work of God.

So liberty can arise from dependence on what Williams calls 'an affirming source', rather than an alien will:

I do not have to be my own origin. I do not have to
try to be a self-creator. There is a level of affirmation
bringing me into and holding me in existence which
I do not have to work for.

We are now a long way from the cliché of seeing
religion as a matter of sucking up to God or staunching
the Creator's anger. Other faiths sum up the matter
in their own ways. Christians may find certain biblical narratives especially liberating, but we have
already noted grounds for seeing interfaith boundaries
as more porous than many suppose.

Much the same could be said for attitudes to moral
formation. Picking up on classical Abrahamic usage –
which in turn matches a central thrust of Hinduism
and Buddhism – innumerable observers have defined
the passions as reflecting surrender to unhealthy appe-
tites. The mistaken or sinful response to temptation
involves instrumentalizing people or things for ego-
tistical gain; the good or holy response invests the
other with due dignity. A large body of spiritual teaching thus warns that uncontrolled passion amounts to
a form of slavery. This much is obvious. A subtler but
no less vital point about human will and choice is that

it can be the least personal thing about us. The major faiths all teach that morality at root has less to do with a supermarket model of choice than with the shaping of desire. Those who have really matured as persons think least about choice. The theologian Peter Groves has glossed this with the example of the Ethiopian famine and Live Aid in 1985. Before the famous Michael Buerk news films exposing the catastrophe to a wider audience, most viewers genuinely didn't know about the epic suffering of entire populations in eastern Africa. They saw it, were moved, and responded. But very quickly they forgot. So another initiative was needed to 'move' them – notably the Live Aid concert, with the harrowing images accompanying it. The venture was very effective. Then people forgot again – after which they dug into their pockets once more during a Christmas appeal. And so the pattern went on. The saint, by contrast, doesn't have to think about doing good, because she or he has become habituated to seeing and responding truthfully.

Buddhism and Christianity offer particularly strong antidotes both to the blunt affirmation of the ego and to the assumption that staking out one's ground as an individual necessarily entails conflict and rivalry. In

Buddhism, progress comes when you grasp the conditioned nature of all events, mental as well as physical. At times this has resulted in an obliviousness of material need, leading to social quietism. For some strands of Buddhism, however, the awareness promotes compassion. Christianity offers the ideal of *apatheia* – the state in which you detach yourself from brute instinct on the one hand and, on the other, channel 'right' passion to overcome the debased sort. Islam, which means both 'submission' and 'peace', preaches an allied message.

On the face of it, the taking of time is a less obvious component of the religious life. But reflection on the meaning of one special day in seven – Fridays for Muslims, the Sabbath for Jews, Sundays for Christians, other days for other believers – offers a signpost. Time is not 'undifferentiated'. Its passing is marked by spiritually pregnant pauses. If you inhabit a religious narrative, time becomes neither just cyclical nor linear. It unfolds, the believer develops, understanding is enlarged. Far from being a commodity, time is seen as a gracious matrix in which believers can both grow and return to the sources of their traditions for further nourishment. This in turn can generate richer approaches to work and well-being. Many on either side of the religion–atheism debate assume that the largest disagreement centres on philosophy and ethics. Perhaps differences over the way time is spent are equally important.

By contrast, mortality is an area where a religious perspective is especially germane given the contemporary instinct to sweep death under the carpet. 'Our mortality tells us that every project we have is limited,' Williams reminds us. 'There is something non-negotiable about that absolute limit' – a point made with force by Ernest Becker in his book *The Denial of Death*.[15] Religion therefore equips the believer to balance attention to the here and now with resignation to death in the longer term.

This is not to say that all in the religious garden is lovely. It would be a colossal overstatement to claim that every believer you or I have ever met is a spiritual athlete radiating a liberating sense of dependence, healthy levels of self-criticism, intellectual openness and serenity in response to time's arrow. The need to distinguish between lofty ideals and often grubby reality when discussing religion at a more general level plainly applies just as much to spiritual practice. The unsettling counterpart of non-disabling dependence is infantilism. Institutions apparently proclaiming release to the captive all too often become repressive. People can try to make their feelings the servants of their wills, with sometimes disastrous results. Ritual understood as a fruitful focus of spiritual energy can become a mechanical end in itself, while some religious language raises anxiety about death and the hereafter rather than watering seeds of hope – or else legitimizes political inertia through peddling pie in the sky.

I have hardly produced a comprehensive conspectus on 'religion' in this chapter. But we are now at least equipped with some criteria allowing us to distinguish between good and bad expressions of it. The really important questions centre on what sort of outlook is being nurtured by the practice of faith. Is it open-handed, outward-looking, conducive to human flourishing in the fullest sense? Is it freely chosen and adaptable without being weak-kneed? Is this all reproduced on a larger scale, namely through the acceptance of pluralism within society?

These questions can in turn form an inspiration and a warning to believers and atheists alike. The former may be challenged to see themselves more as others see them; the latter to view religion as amounting to something rather different from assent to dubious propositions.

3

Bad faith, good faith

The thesis that religion does more good than harm, being a set of overlapping and broadly positive principles and practices, has been eloquently summarized by Keith Ward:

God is not some sort of arbitrary tyrant . . . [but rather] is apprehended as one who has a purpose in creation, and who gives human beings a part to play in realising that purpose. The purpose of God is . . . that societies of finite personal beings should . . . grow in knowledge and understanding, in synergy and empathy with one another, and in the creation and appreciation of the beauty and intricate structure of the world. This is a growth towards greater conscious appreciation of love, beauty and truth.[1]

Those with doubts about such a sunny assessment may counter that it is too abstract. Given that faith communities are always culturally embedded, you are unlikely to convince the doubters by relying on free-floating statements. Sociological spadework is needed to give the insights expressed by defenders of religion a securer foundation – and also to unearth some flaws in their arguments. A good example of Ward's misguided approach is his idea that Islam, as a monotheistic faith without incarnational belief, essentially resembles an offshoot of Christianity such as Unitarianism.[2] Islam's monistic picture of God is certainly shared by Unitarians in some respects. The point of our ground-clearing so far has been to demonstrate that this and other conceptions can indeed be reasonable and fruitful in theory. But we are still some way from establishing whether this or that faith does more harm than good *in practice*. On the fundamental question of attitudes to violence, for example, Islam and Christianity are not the same.

A broader view of the landscape comes in the work of a figure like David Martin, who grasps in effect that the difficulties implicit in Ward's arguments mirror those in the New Atheist camp. Richard Dawkins,

Christopher Hitchens, Philip Pullman and other god-less standard-bearers avoid argumentative subtlety through an identification of evil with religion as such. So the 'proof' that religion causes violence is seen as a simple matter of identifying 'facts' such as the Crusades. Again, little or no effort is made to lay bare the social channels through which religion is filtered. Pullman's linking of evil with 'the Authority' – namely religion in light fictional disguise – is even more telling. The vision grows from a large seam of politics that proclaims innocence and pins all that is toxic on a particular structure – capitalism or patriarchy, say – which must be eliminated. We are not a million miles from the saving conflagrations of Marxist rhetoric here. Destroy in order to save.

Dawkins's weakness is reflected in his revealing assumption that 'true' science can be distinguished from sordid examples of abuse on the ground. The truth, in Robert Bellah's memorable expression, is that there is no perfume without mustard gas. We have also noted that scientific knowledge put to good account in curing disease can assist the torturer in causing even greater pain. As Martin has argued, if Christianity can be blamed for Torquemada, then physics must carry the can for nuclear weapons, sociology for neo-Darwinian eugenics, and the Enlightenment for Stalin. Despite their protestations of innocence or objectivity, the Enlightenment's secular heirs themselves stand in a tradition steeped in the language of utopian violence. If you doubt this, just consult the lyrics of the Marseillaise.

Religion cannot be let off the hook for its own malign influences either. For example, the argument that Christianity has not aggravated the persecution of gay people – on the basis that all past societies have been homophobic[3] – will puzzle a large number of believers and unbelievers alike. True, many societies around the world have demonized same-sex relationships. But Judeo-Christianity has provided strong buttressing down the ages for a damaging prejudice. Does that make Christianity inherently homophobic, though? Not necessarily. Burrow down into Scripture and tradition, and you may conclude that there is a credible revisionist case for gay equality.[4] You may also judge that the Bible is not clear enough to settle the matter – that Christian resources are thus themselves problematic. Or that the sacred text needs dethroning to some extent, or at least setting within a broader biblical context. Or simply that centuries of homophobia can be substantially explained by a combination of ignorance in pre-modern societies and a lack of charity. Another vexed question is the immense trauma caused by hellfire teaching in church and mosque. Does the problem lie with wooden interpretations of ambiguous texts (the Greek word *gehenna*, which is translated as 'hell' in the Gospels, was a burning rubbish dump near Jerusalem)? Is it respectable to decide from a reading of the New Testament as a whole that 'hell' is more synonymous with resistance to God's love? Does this reading in turn point to the prospect of universal reconciliation or *apokatastasis* – and thus to the belief that hell will ultimately be an empty place? Or are the teachings of Jesus, as his critics hold, just ambiguous?

In other words, *pace* both Ward and the New Atheists, broad-brush respect or disrespect for a tradition may play well to a particular constituency, but is nevertheless debatable when viewed in the round. From this follow some important lessons, including that Kant and others have been wrong to see 'religion' as an isolable kernel of moral truth awkwardly encased in mythology, despite the similarities between major traditions that we have noted. To corroborate the point further, let us look in more detail at the positions occupied by this or that faith on a spectrum of options vis-à-vis worldliness.

Like Islam, Christianity is on one level saturated in the language of victory. But one way of encapsulating the difference has been as follows. The Christian vision is of triumph *over* the world, while Islam enjoins victory *in* it. Eye-for-an-eye morality – although itself an advance on disproportionate retaliation – is repudiated even more comprehensively in Christianity than in either Judaism or Islam. Neither the Hebrew Bible nor the Qur'an goes quite as far as enjoining believers to turn the other cheek, though the Scriptures of all three faiths include the immensely important story of Joseph/Yussuf, seen as an emblem of self-giving love.[5] The Qur'an contains injunctions rising above the *lex talionis* – for example, 'Withhold your hand' (from self-defence against persecution), 4.77. Yet the difference between Jesus and Muhammad is stark in some respects. Jesus entered Jerusalem unarmed, riding a donkey, before going on to convert the city and its Temple into his own spiritual body. Muhammad took Mecca at the head of an army, arguably calling on his followers to effect global conquest. To repeat: I am not denying the worldliness of many Christians. The language of Islam, especially in the Sufi tradition, can be world-renouncing, while that of Constantinian Christianity has sometimes resembled Islam's realism about political power, especially when Christendom was at its zenith during the Middle Ages. Furthermore, the Churches have often looked both ways, at times endorsing the self-subversive vision of the Gospels, while regularly settling for alliances with secular power. Mary became patroness of cities and countries, while the cross was being recast as a sword. But the appropriation was far from total. Monarchs and popes washed the feet of the poor in Holy Week; Christian vocabulary is used to dethrone the powers that be, ecclesiastical as well as temporal, in *The Divine Comedy* among many other texts.

Some commentators are reluctant to think in broad, quasi-abstract terms, pointing out that, for centuries and in many regions of the world, Sufism was the majority version of Islam. If we *were* to propose general conclusions avoiding undue caricature, however, a credible thesis would be that both religions include ascetic forms of spirituality that could be described as seeking 'victory over the world', and both also include political ambitions. Islam has its *Umma*. But it was precisely because Christianity proved so successful in creating an alternative civil society within the Roman Empire that it moved so seamlessly to becoming a governing partner of the state after Constantine. Perhaps, then, the fundamental difference is that Christianity's political ambitions do not, *in theory*, allow for violence, while Islam's do. For example, although both faiths have their saintly ascetics, Sufi masters have throughout history taken up the sword in religio-political defence of Islam; and though Christianity has had its prince-bishops, they were rarely renowned for their holiness. Saintly monks who were also warriors have not been unknown, especially during the Crusades. But they have been fewer in number. A better way of framing the contrast could be to say that, politically, Christianity is a civil society that became a state, and Islam is a state that became a civil society. But remember the variables. The Churches have changed much over the past century; Islam, too, is constantly evolving; what we think of as Islam has in any case been shaped by the adverse legacy of colonialism and the dismantling of social and religious ecosystems by Western invaders.

Significantly, the notion of the world against which Christianity pitches itself is precisely what ushers in a sense of the secular. Jesus himself separates the things of Caesar and those of God, a contrast echoed in Augustine's two-cities model, among many other sources. We have already instanced Magna Carta and the work of Milton as biblically based catalysts for social progress; a complex lineage is traced with assurance in the work of Larry Siedentop. The roots of liberalism, he argues,

> were firmly established in the arguments of philosophers and canon lawyers by the fourteenth and early fifteenth centuries: belief in a fundamental equality of status as the proper basis for a legal system; belief that enforcing moral conduct is a contradiction in terms; a defence of individual liberty, through the assertion of fundamental 'natural' rights; and, finally, the conclusion that only a representative form of government is appropriate for a society resting on the assumption of moral equality.[6]

At the same time, and given the human realities I have described, every radical vision will generate ideas both supportive and subversive of power. What is true of

Christianity or Enlightenment liberalism or Marxism is just as true of Buddhism. I have no wish to question the richness of the Buddhist vision at its best, or the immense fruit it has borne in the lives of countless people. The Eightfold Path – including right speech, right action and right mindfulness – speaks for itself. Our concern is not just with inspiring values, however, but with problematic outcomes in the public square. Buddhism's non-hierarchical structure – the very reason for its appeal to many in the contemporary West – is also the source of damaging cloudiness. The darker side of this apparently most peaceable of faiths is set out in sometimes alarming detail in the essay collection *Buddhist Warfare.*[7] This text tells us of the 'Soldier-Zen' mode, and of massacres carried out by the Buddhist cult army at Faqing 1,500 years ago. A soldier who killed another man was judged to have achieved the dignity of bodhisattva or Buddha-to-be. More killing equated to greater advancement along this track. The fighters were given a drug that removed all inhibitions: fathers and sons murdered one another without compunction.

Is this tragic aberration liable to arise from time to time in all cultures, especially when narcotics are involved? Probably; but the matter cannot be laid to rest with a shrug. The atrocity just outlined was justified with reference to the core Buddhist teaching of no-self. Consider views expressed by the seventeenth-century Zen Master Takuan, for example:

> The uplifted sword has not will of its own, it is all of emptiness. It is like a flash of lightning. The man who is about to be struck down is also of emptiness, and so is the one who wields the sword. None of them is possessed of a mind that has any substantiality. As each of them is of emptiness and has no 'mind', the striking man is not a man, the sword in his hand is not a sword, and the 'I' who is about to be struck down is like the splitting of the spring breeze in a flash of lightning.[8]

Nor can the connection between Zen and violence be consigned to the remote past. Military training before and during the Asia-Pacific War, in which 20 million Chinese perished, was heavily marked by Soldier-Zen philosophy and especially by the influence of D. T. Suzuki (1870–1966). Some might associate figures such as Suzuki with later distortions of fundamental Buddhist texts. This, too, is disingenuous – perhaps because Buddhism is unduly influenced by Taoism, with its own ambiguous emphasis on the law of nature. The seventh-century Chan text 'Treatise on Absolute Contemplation' displays a marked debt to Taoism:

> Question: 'In certain conditions, isn't one allowed to kill a living being?' Answer: 'The brush fire burns the mountain; the hurricane breaks trees; the collapsing cliff crushes wild animals to death; the running mountain stream drowns insects. If a man can make his mind similar [to such forces], then, meeting a man, he may kill him all the same.'[9]

The examples could be multiplied. Katherine Wharton, a scholar of Buddhism, instances the Heap of Jewels sutra, translated into Chinese as far back as the second century CE. In it a disciple, Manjushri, menaces the Buddha with a sword. 'The Buddha then praises him for this,' Wharton writes, because '"there isn't any more of me than there is of anyone else. If Manjushri were to kill the Buddha it would have been a right killing."'[10]

From this we can draw an important moral: that since 'emptiness' is a hazy goal, it is questionable to claim that one who has achieved it is incapable of violence. Why assume that such a state – which includes the acceptance of contingency and the denial of personal identity – is synonymous with the renunciation of power relations when it can equally well be held to reflect the cruelty of nature? And why in any case should the renunciation of power relations be seen as good in itself? A flawed world entails an inherent tension between peace and justice. That was the insight animating a host of thinkers from St Augustine, an early framer of Christian just-war thinking, to opponents of appeasement during the 1930s. In traditional Mahayana Buddhism a stress on emptiness is qualified by karma – the notion that good generates more good and bad more bad. But many contemporary Buddhists see belief about cosmic justice as passé.[11] In my view, they are over-invested in 'emptiness'. It is naive to equate emptiness with compassion pure and simple: excess freight is being attached to a tricky idea. Combine a contentious basic term with a very varied reception history, and you have a challenge. As a Christian, I am attracted to Buddhism on several levels. But I write as a candid friend of a tradition with an uneven record, in theory as well as practice.

Readers may query the rationale for spelling out problems with Buddhism at some length given that the Churches have also regularly claimed a theological warrant for violence or intolerance. The difference is that Christianity's message, despite the corruptions, is more focused – both through the historical authenticity and weight of the Gospels themselves and because the mainstream Churches have stronger structures of authority, making it easier to distinguish right from wrong interpretation and action. The dynamics of the Christian life on the ground are not always smoother, just somewhat easier to calibrate – even if sometimes institutional strength is precisely the problem. For example, the Vatican has rightly drawn heavy criticism for hushing up clerical child abuse. So, aside from the fundamentals of a given faith, the balance struck between clarity of message on the one hand, and institutional transparency on the other, emerges as a salient yardstick for judging how much good or harm it does. As it happens, an important strand in papal history over recent centuries has been *resistance* to meddling by the secular power. The pitfalls of over-centralization are obvious, but a contrary menace should also be taken into account. In Russia, the

Orthodox Church has long been a department of state, and thus a mouthpiece for government propaganda. Elsewhere within the household of faith, evangelical Protestants in the USA regularly transmit their message through a nationalist lens. In other religions, authority also tends to be highly dispersed.

What I have said at some length about Buddhism applies in comparable ways to Hinduism. There is a certain match (noted already) between India's largest spiritual grouping and the Abrahamic religions at a conceptual level. Yet Hinduism does not constitute a creed as such, or even necessarily a religion as conceived elsewhere. It is a commonplace that even to speak of Hindu theology represents the imposition of foreign categories on a highly diffuse set of beliefs and rituals. A common interpretation of this inchoate faith is that it evolved from the pantheism and animism of Aryan settlers into a pantheon swallowing up a host of religious cults. Those who see deeper unity beneath the diversity (including devotees of a philosophical school such as Advaita Vedanta) tend to emphasize a common commitment to the oneness of all reality. The main point for our purposes is that, despite the good also done by Hindus, the colossal evil of the caste system remains embedded in what will soon be the world's most populous nation.

We have also seen that religious minorities in the subcontinent are suffering rising violence at the hands of nationalist firebrands insistent that Indian and Hindu identities are inseparable. It is hard to tell zealots that they have betrayed the tenets of their faith if it is too baggy to define in the first place. Shashi Tharoor has recently voiced a *cri de cœur* about the corruption of 'true' – that is, tolerant, undogmatic – Hinduism by supporters of a demagogue such as Narendra Modi. Tharoor poses a pointed question: 'How dare a bunch of thugs shrink the soaring majesty of the Vedas and the *Upanishads* to the petty bigotry of their brand of identity politics?'[12] Though Tharoor certainly commands sympathy, he is vulnerable to a counter-charge. If a given community starts with an open door (the Charvaka School even incorporates atheism into a Hindu framework), then it should not be surprised by the appearance of unwelcome visitors. 'Tolerance' can sometimes be so elastic as to include its opposite.

Perhaps the most pressing topic to be faced in these pages is that of contemporary Islamist violence, and what it says about the martial aspects of Islam. Many Muslim-majority societies are plainly in ferment. Despite grave errors in Western policy towards Iraq in particular, the blame for this strife cannot be laid on the shoulders of foreign agents alone. Iran and Saudi Arabia are battling each other aggressively via proxies.

Two influential responses to all this evidence, along with a torrent of terrorist atrocities on several continents, strike me as mistaken. One, associated with conservative polemicists, sees the bloodshed as reflecting a pure – indeed, the most orthodox – form of Islam. This view betrays ignorance of Muslim thought in the round. The other, voiced by one-sided commentators on the other side of the argument, plays down the religious factor in relation to others. Since there is so much else that propels the terrorist, according to one proponent of this view – 'the role of social networks and family ties; issues of identity and belonging; a sense of persecution; mental illness; socio-economic grievances; moral outrage over conflict and torture; a craving for glory and purpose, action and adventure' – faith can be discounted as a driving force.[13] Wrong. When a militant screaming

'Allahu Akbar' drives a lorry into the path of shoppers, common sense suggests that a religious narrative has galvanized the other elements listed above. Read Mark Juergensmeyer's *Terror in the Mind of God*, a survey of rising religious violence around the globe, and you see the ingredients – political, certainly, but also irreducibly theological – animating a figure such as Mahmud Abouhalima, one of the conspirators behind the 1993 bombing of the World Trade Center.[14] He is hardly untypical of his kind.

Those who think that Islam represents a less acceptable face of religion tend to quote this or that passage from the Qur'an out of context in support of their claims. The command to kill idolaters (sura 9:5) is widely rehearsed. More searching questions are overlooked, notably why Muslim societies have on the whole been better than their Christian counterparts at absorbing minorities (at least before the twentieth century); and why the vast majority of Muslims, yesterday and today, have no truck with violent extremism. A large part of the answer is that relevant passages of the Qur'an – like verses in Hebrew Scripture that represent God as violent or vengeful – have been contextualized by a sophisticated body of reflection. Some Qur'anic passages are considered permanently binding; others relate to specific circumstances in which Muhammad's early followers were under military threat. For this reason the practice of jihad was regulated. Its lawful expressions do not include terrorist violence. This does not mean that politicians such as Barack Obama, desperate to paint Islam as 'a religion of peace', have been right to discount the Islamic element in Islamist violence. Violent jihadists resemble Christian fundamentalists in leap-frogging schools of interpretation through a regression to 'unmediated' Scripture.

Today's crisis in the Muslim world derives from Wahhabism, the puritanical strain of the faith that arose in eighteenth-century Arabia in opposition to notionally idolatrous practices such as praying at the shrines of holy men. Wahhabism in turn draws inspiration from Ibn Taymiyya, the fourteenth-century cleric who was widely criticized in his day. We have seen that the broader Islamic landscape is much richer. One might cite an Arab-Muslim humanist tradition dating back at least to the tenth century. Thinkers in the Greco-Arabic constellation contributed greatly to scholastic philosophy. The jurisprudential schools of the Muslim world display great pliancy.

Wahhabism has spread for reasons including Saudi Arabia's economic importance. Before the discovery of oil there, the peninsula was a relative backwater. Wahhabists and Salafists have sidelined other forms of Islam in the Saudi kingdom: among other severe measures they have replaced the four pulpits at the base of the Kabba in Mecca (each representing a school of Sunni Islam) with a single one for the exclusive use of Wahhabi preachers. They have abolished the veneration of saints, destroying shrines used by other Sunnis as well as Shias. Conflating Wahhabists with Islam is thus as unjust as confusing Christianity with the Inquisition. The late Shahab Ahmed's baggy but important book *What is Islam?*[15] traces an immensely rich cultural genealogy in what the author terms the Balkans to Bengal strand of the faith: tolerant, undogmatic, hospitable to science and other forms of secular learning, unfazed by wine-drinking and erotic – including homoerotic – verse.

Though very important, however, a textured awareness of Islam does not serve to sweep away legitimate questions about the world's fastest-growing faith. The caveats spelt out above must be balanced by recognition that Islam is a theocratic project programmed for success. Since Muslim pre-eminence was assumed during the evolution of Islamic law, virtually no Muslim-majority society has ever treated non-Muslim citizens on terms of full equality. Turkey today retains its Ottoman stamp by restricting Christians, Shia Muslims and other minorities in numerous ways.[16] Conversion from Islam to other faiths in Muslim-majority societies can be highly perilous: sharia law prescribes harsh punishments for women and even more severe penalties for men. The 'blasphemy' laws are being grotesquely abused in several Muslim countries, especially Pakistan – a disaster portrayed with power and lyricism by Nadeem Aslam in his novel *The Golden Legend*.[17] The debate in France between Gilles Kepel, who talks of *Islam radicalisé*, and Olivier Roy, whose emphasis is on *radicalisme islamé*, brings focus to this subject. Both are right up to a point: to see this is to get beyond the rigid dichotomy of 'Islam is inherently violent' versus 'Islam is a religion of peace'.

The wisest prescription for Islam in my view is not that it needs a Reformation. It has been undergoing a Reformation of sorts for over 200 years. The results have been as blood-soaked as the European Reformation. Rather, Muslims would be well advised to excavate resources that are already available. This was the path taken by progressive Catholics (Joseph Ratzinger among them) eager to regenerate an often stagnant ecclesiastical culture before the Second Vatican Council of 1962–5.

Just as Christianity has evolved through fertile engagement both with its own traditions and those of wider society, there are grounds for hope that Islam will develop in analogous ways. But we have registered that Islam lacks the structures of authority that would make it easier to rein in extremism. No Muslim cleric has the influence of a pope. For this and other reasons glanced at, the process is unlikely to be smooth. The tools exist, but they want repairing. It seems right nevertheless to finish on an irenic note by re-emphasizing that the points of contact between the two faiths are at least as significant as the differences. When they are true to their guiding principles, both insist on the sanctity of the person as a seeker of God, and from this should duly follow a recognition of religious freedom as the first of human rights.

Some secularists may still see this as an essentially defensive argument. In other words, given the tendency of human beings to cling to their mythologies, then the least worst option is to accentuate the positive. But for the undeceived, of course, humanism pure and simple remains the truest path. I have already suggested that this stance is vulnerable to attack, partly because secular visions of the good life often borrow from theology without due recognition – and thus reject religious resources at their peril.[18] Consider a vivid example. Philosophers standing in the liberal tradition of John Stuart Mill have enormous problems with examples including a voluntary gladiatorial contest. We could note that there are people who will engage in such combat for a sufficiently large sum of money, with an assurance that the millions earned will go to their family if they lose. The spectacle would only be available to paying customers behind high fences. What would be wrong with that on libertarian grounds? For the strict secularist, it is very difficult to say. It is likewise very difficult to spell out what is wrong with bestiality on libertarian grounds. The only way to do so would be by holding that it is incompatible with a strong sense of the dignity of the person. Ever since Kant, opinion-formers have been trying to give a 'rational' account of such dignity without theological underpinnings. The political philosopher

Andrea Sangiovanni has recently tried to do this in *Humanity without Dignity*,[19] but many are unconvinced by his arguments. You still require a sense that there is some value that cannot be fully explicated in purely naturalistic terms. In essence, human rights discourse cannot be disembedded from broader philosophical – and theological – traditions. Rights divorced from an innate sense of human dignity can easily descend into a battle over rival entitlements. (It could be added in passing that if civil society is ever fully secured in China, it will have much to do with the vast spiritual revival now unfolding in a land where religion was said to have been expunged as recently as the 1970s. The moral desert left by Mao is gradually showing signs of new life.[20])

Another problem with secularism worth sketching in brief is its own gods – all the more detrimental, perhaps, because they are not even recognized as such. Tom Wright among others has observed that nature abhors a vacuum (philosophical as much as physical), and that three pagan deities from antiquity – Mars the god of war, Mammon the god of money, and Aphrodite, goddess of erotic love – are still worshipped in fresh guises. Explicitly so, in fact, since the hermeneutics of suspicion set out by Nietzsche, Marx and Freud respectively locate fundamental human urges in the will to power, economic drives, and sex. Wright's verdict is telling:

> Our society, claiming to have got rid of God upstairs so that we can live our lives the way we want . . . has in fact fallen back into the clutches of forces . . . that are bigger than ourselves, more powerful than the sum total of people who give them allegiance – forces we might as well recognize as gods.[21]

Granted all these factors, a viable conclusion in three parts is that religion does more harm than good when its practitioners are intolerant or violent. Religious bodies are not incapable of error; their representatives can easily make statements going far beyond the basic natural perception of the mystery of existence. Such statements can lead to mistakes, conflict and other evils, including the idolization of community identities. In certain respects, the history of religion maps on to the entire social history of humanity. The problem is especially felt in significant sections of the Muslim, Hindu and Buddhist worlds today; Christian societies were deeply marked by such stains as recently as the

1930s and 1940s but are now on the whole much more tolerant: true to a combination of their direct roots, and to secular Enlightenment – soil itself partly watered by Judeo-Christianity. Two conspicuous exceptions are the Russian Orthodox Church, the leaders of which are under the thumb of Vladimir Putin; and the American fundamentalists who oppose science and legitimate political diversity.

The second part of this verdict could be that religion does more good than harm when it evinces love of neighbour – especially when definitions of neighbour are stretched to include the stranger – through magnanimity towards other belief systems, as well as feeding the hungry and clothing the naked. Secularists tend to take their creed too much for granted, forgetting its theological underpinnings. Reason can transport us to the domain of prudence; it is the spiritual dimension that can advance us further, towards goals including grace and forgiveness.

Score draw? Not quite. Third, and ultimately, I think that religion does more good than harm because, like science or music, we need it. Tone-deaf people can go through life without delighting in songs or symphonies. But most of us feel enriched by music at some level. You can shun technology by going to live in an Amish-style commune; the majority would avoid such a drastic step. Religion is the most contested element of this triad. But most people in most cultures, present as well as past, would accept my premise. Beyond this stands an especially important notion – that human understanding is not exhausted by mapping the world of nature. People will always ask larger questions about what the good life consists in. And through seeking answers, they will stumble upon moments, places, relationships and experiences that have a numinous character – 'as though removed from this world and in some way casting judgment upon it',[22] in Roger Scruton's resonant expression.

For pastors and other spiritual leaders, the need is for public expressions of faith that are broad enough to be inclusive, fostering the ability to live and move within a given spiritual heritage and not be narrowed by it, but also firm enough to be rooted in what has been received from the past, and to cast necessary judgement on the spirit of the age where appropriate. Though the vision is not easy to implement in every particular, it can nevertheless be spelt out with rea- sonable clarity in headline terms. Conviction and dogmatism are not the same. There is a difference between having seen some truth and claiming to speak in the name of all truth; between knowing what one believes and refusing to respect the beliefs and experiences of others. People of faith should speak with a humble authority combining real knowledge with an awareness of the limitations of that knowledge. Their authority, to coin a powerful image used by John Habgood a generation ago, is not that of the wise woman or man and the scholar, important though wisdom and scholarship are, but that of lovers who express their delight in what they love, even though they have scarcely begun to glimpse its full extent.

Notes

1 Grasping the question

1 Christopher Hitchens, *God Is Not Great: How Religion Poisons Everything* (London: Atlantic Books, 2007).

2 Tim Crane, *The Meaning of Belief: Religion from an Atheist's Point of View* (Cambridge, MA: Harvard University Press, 2017), p. 138.

3 Rupert Shortt, *Christianophobia: A Faith under Attack* (London: Rider, 2012), Introduction.

4 Raymond Aron, *Peace and War: A Theory of International Relations* (London: Transaction, 2003).

5 William T. Cavanaugh, *The Myth of Religious Violence* (Oxford: Oxford University Press, 2010).

6 Sarah Eltantawi, *Shar'iah on Trial: Northern Nigeria's Islamic Revolution* (Oakland, CA: University of California Press, 2017).

7 Richard Dawkins, *The God Delusion* (London: Black Swan, 2006), pp. 180ff.

8 The anecdote is told in Oliver Sacks's memoir, *Uncle Tungsten* (New York: Vintage, 2001).

2 Spiritual paths in theory and practice

1 For an overview of the landscape see, for example, Timothy Samuel Shah and Monica Duffy Toft, 'Why God Is Winning', *Foreign Policy*, 9 June 2006, <www.foreignpolicy.com>. Appendix A of Rupert Shortt, *Christianophobia: A Faith under Attack* (London: Rider, 2012) draws on information collated about freedom of belief around the world – often described as the canary in the coalmine for the prospering of a society more generally. Of the 41 countries judged free in religious terms – that is, scoring 1, 2 or 3 on a scale of 1 to 7 – 35 are traditionally Christian. Only 2 traditionally Christian countries out of 45, Belarus and Cuba, were deemed to

be 'not free' – that is, scoring a 6 or a 7. The other countries rated highly included three traditionally Buddhist domains: Japan, Mongolia and Thailand. Buddhist societies scoring poorly were those with Communist governments: China, Tibet, Laos, North Korea and Vietnam. Among the small number of Hindu-majority countries, Nepal scored poorly on both political and religious freedom, while India, unusually, was rated highly in the former category, and badly in the latter. This apparent anomaly is usually ascribed to the growth of Hindutva over recent decades. Muslim-majority states scored poorly for the most part, though religiously free Islamic polities do exist – Senegal, for example.

2 I have tried to give a sense of the recovery of nerve in theology – not least by basking in the reflected glory of some leading exponents – in Rupert Shortt (ed.), *God's Advocates: Christian Thinkers in Conversation* (London: Darton, Longman & Todd, 2005).

3 *The modal ontological argument.* At its plainest, the ontological argument maintains that God exists because God has maximal greatness by definition, and maximal greatness necessarily entails existence. Among the most famous objections to this are that existence is not a predicate like size or shape, say. I agree with David Bentley Hart that though the weight of philosophical opinion is against this 'proof', it has partial value in alerting us to the uniqueness of 'necessary' existence. God is not to be thought of as a thing among other things. A recent variation on the argument employs modal logic: 'There is a possible world in which God exists, and a deity existing in a possible world must by definition exist in all worlds, actual as well as possible.' Speculation about the metaphysical status of possible worlds takes us into arcane territory. Nevertheless, those who reject this line of reasoning outright are forced into the difficult position of claiming that God could not possibly exist (a very tall order indeed when one reflects on the sheer scope of what is logically possible).

4 *The kalām cosmological argument.* Popularized in the present by thinkers including William Lane Craig, but also drawing on medieval Islamic sources, this rests on claims about the impossibility

of actually existing infinities. It differs from the versions of the cosmological argument advanced by St Thomas Aquinas, who urges that an endless 'hierarchical' sequence of causes is impossible, and Leibniz, whose focus is on the Principle of Sufficient Reason.

5 *The argument from moral truths.* One can naturally deny that there are objective moral truths with a Nietzschean move (i.e. nihilism), or else claim with Plato that such truths do exist but float free of a theistic anchor, but this stance poses substantial difficulties.

6 *The argument from mathematical truths.* Mathematical objects are not natural objects, so naturalism cannot explain them. But science seems to presuppose their existence. The two alternatives to a theistic solution are 'fictionalism' and 'Platonism' – there are plausible cases to be made for these, but in the end I think the objections they face are much worse than explaining them in terms of God's creative blueprint for physical reality.

7 *The argument from fine-tuning.* I still think this is a powerful one, not least because it is motivated by the best available cosmological evidence.

8 *The argument from consciousness.* This depends on accepting that mental states are not identical with or reducible to physical states. Many – including even some analytic philosophers – take the common-sense view that consciousness is real and irreducible.

9 David Bentley Hart, *The Experience of God: Being, Consciousness, Bliss* (New Haven, CT: Yale University Press, 2013), p. 44.

10 See, for example, Peter E. Hodgson, *Theology and Modern Physics* (Abingdon: Routledge, 2005).

11 Jonathan Benthall, in conversation with the author.

12 Clare Carlisle, reviewing Tim Crane, *The Meaning of Belief,* in *The Times Literary Supplement* (*TLS*), 17 November 2017, <www.thetls.co.uk>.

13 Jonathan Sacks, 'The Pope is Right about the Threat to Freedom', *The Times,* 3 February 2010, <www.thetimes.co.uk>.

14 See, for example, Rowan Williams, 'Faith and Human Flourishing:

Religious Beliefs and Ideals of Maturity', an Oxford University Podcast, uploaded on 12 February 2014, <https://podcasts.ox. ac.uk>. The quotations in the paragraph that follows are from the same source.

15 Ernest Becker, *The Denial of Death* (New York and London: Free Press, 1997).

3 Bad faith, good faith

1 Keith Ward, *Is Religion Dangerous?* (London: Lion, 2006), p. 137.
2 Ward, *Is Religion Dangerous?*, pp. 185ff.
3 Ward, *Is Religion Dangerous?*, pp. 124ff.
4 See, for example, Eugene Rogers, *Theology and Sexuality: Classic and Contemporary Readings* (Oxford: Wiley-Blackwell, 2001).
5 The parallels are spelt out by Kenneth Cragg, a pioneer of Christian–Muslim dialogue, in *The Iron in the Soul: Joseph and the Undoing of Violence* (London: Melisende, 2009).
6 Larry Siedentop, *Inventing the Individual: The Origins of Western Liberalism* (London: Allen Lane, 2014), p. 332. For an especially illuminating discussion of this passage, and a refutation of Steven Pinker's neglect of Christianity's role in fomenting progress, see Nick Spencer, www.theosthinktank.co.uk/comment/2018/02/20/ enlightenment-and-progress-or-why-steven-pinker-is-wrong.
7 Michael K. Jerryson and Mark Juergensmeyer, eds, *Buddhist Warfare* (Oxford and New York: Oxford University Press, 2010).
8 For a bracing discussion of this passage, see Katherine Wharton, *TLS*, 1 October 2010, <www.the-tls.co.uk>.
9 Jerryson and Juergensmeyer, *Buddhist Warfare*, p. 123.
10 Wharton, *TLS*, 1 October 2010, <www.the-tls.co.uk>.
11 See, for example, Dale Wright, *The Six Imperfections: Buddhism and the Cultivation of Character* (Oxford and New York: Oxford University Press, 2010).
12 Shashi Tharoor, *Why I am a Hindu* (London: Hurst, 2018), p. 252.
13 Medhi Hasan, <www.theintercept.com>, 29 March 2017.
14 Mark Juergensmeyer, *Terror in the Mind of God: The Global Rise*

of Religious Violence (Oakland, CA: University of California Press, 2003), pp. 78ff.

15 Shahab Ahmed, *What is Islam? The Importance of Being Islamic* (Princeton, NJ: Princeton University Press, 2015).

16 See Rupert Shortt, *Christianophobia: A Faith under Attack* (London: Rider, 2012), pp. 87ff., for a detailed discussion of Turkey's poor record on religious freedom.

17 Nadeem Aslam, *The Golden Legend* (London: Faber & Faber, 2017).

18 Consider, for example, the very thought-provoking reflections of Jacques Maritain in *The Rights of Man and Natural Law*, translated by Doris C. Anson (New York: Gordian Press, 1971), pp. 21–2: 'Finally the conception of society we are describing is *theist* or *Christian*, not in the sense that it would require every member of society to believe in God and to be Christian, but in the sense that it recognizes that in the reality of things, God, principle and end of the human person and prime source of natural law, is by the same token the prime source of political society and authority among men; and in the sense that it recognizes that the currents of liberty and fraternity released by the Gospel, the virtues of justice and friendship sanctioned by it, the practical respect for the human person proclaimed by it, the feeling of responsibility before God required by it, as from him who exercises the authority as from him who is subject to it, are the internal energy which civilization needs to achieve its fulfilment.'

19 Andrea Sangiovanni, *Humanity without Dignity: Moral Equality, Respect, and Human Rights* (Cambridge, MA: Harvard University Press, 2017).

20 China's transformation is chronicled in detail by Ian Johnson in *The Souls of China: The Return of Religion after Mao* (London: Allen Lane, 2017).

21 Tom Wright, *Surprised by Scripture* (London: SPCK, 2013), p. 155.

22 Roger Scruton, *The Spectator*, 31 May 2014.

Index